Sophia

God Bless You!

Love, The Buddy Family

A Child's First Book of Prayers

Lois Rock

illustrated by Alison Jay

The illustrations in this book were selected from The Classic Treasury of Children's Prayers, published by Augsburg Fortress in 2000

Written and compiled by Lois Rock
Illustrations copyright © 1999 Alison Jay
This edition copyright © 2002 Lion Publishing

First Augsburg Books edition. Originally published as A Child's First Book of Prayers copyright © 2002, Lion Publishing plc, Mayfield House, 256 Banbury Road, Oxford OX2 7DH England
www.lion-publishing.co.uk

ISBN 0-8066-4374-9
AF 9-4374

First edition 2002. All rights reserved.

Printed and bound in Singapore
4 5 6 7 8 9 10

Acknowledgments
Every effort has been made to trace and contact copyright owners for material used in this book. We apologize for any inadvertent omissions or errors.

All unattributed prayers by Lois Rock, copyright © Lion Publishing. Thank You for the Firefighters by Victoria Tebbs (p. 54) copyright © Lion Publishing. Summer Sky of Blue and White by Mary Joslin (p. 90) copyright © Lion Publishing. A Pentecost Prayer (p. 138) copyright © Lion Publishing. Material from The Alternative Service Book, 1980 (p. 158) is copyright © The Archbishop's Council. Extract reproduced by permission. Who Made the Night-time Shadows? and Tucked up in My Little Bed by Sophie Piper (pp. 200 & 204) copyright © Lion Publishing. Preserve Us, O Lord, while Waking (p. 209) from The Prayer Book as Proposed in 1928 and reproduced in Lent, Holy Week, and Easter is copyright © The Central Board of Finance of the Church of England 1984, 1986; The Archbishop's Council 1999 and is reproduced by permission. Scripture quotations on pp. 88, 146, 147, 149, 150, 151, 154, 155, 156 and 160 quoted from the Good News Bible published by The Bible Societies/HarperCollins Publishers Ltd, UK © American Bible Society 1966, 1971, 1976, 1992, used with permission.

Introduction

Learning to pray is learning to see the world as it looks from heaven. It means learning to believe in the power of faith and hope and love… the unfailing love of God.

May these simple prayers be a first step in your journey.

Contents

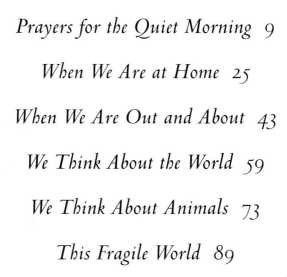

Prayers
for the
Quiet
Morning

Through the night thy angels kept
Watch above me while I slept;
Now the dark has passed away,
Thank thee, Lord, for this new day.

William Canton

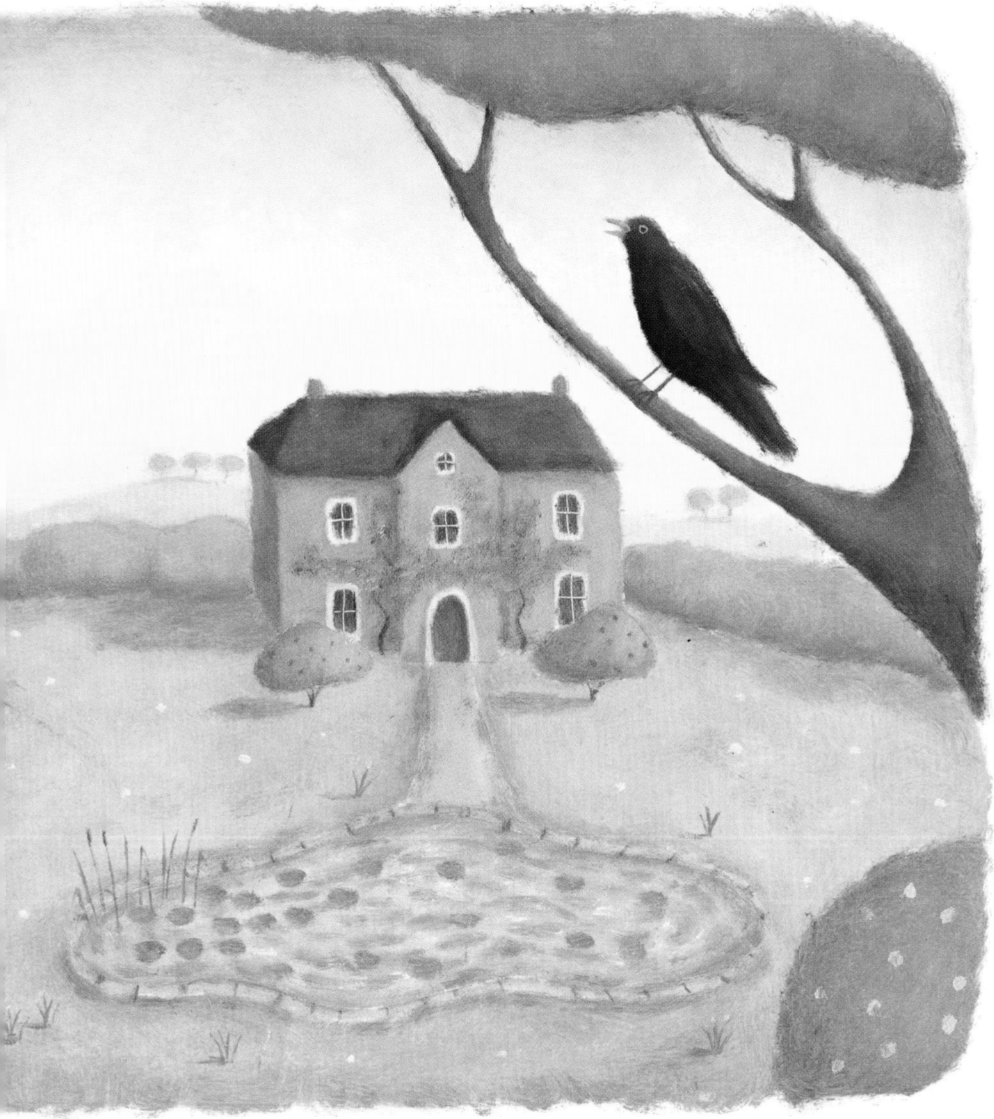

Thank you, God in heaven,
For a day begun.
Thank you for the breezes,
Thank you for the sun.
For this time of gladness,
For our work and play,
Thank you, God in heaven,
For another day.

Traditional

Thank you for this new day.
May I bring to it something good.
May I make of it something good.
May I take from it something good.

O let us feel you very near
When we kneel down to pray.
Let us be still that you may send
A message for today.

Anonymous

Dear God,

It is easier to believe you are near

when the world is quiet.

Help us to know you are near

when it grows noisy.

Quietly, in the morning,
I rise and look at the sky
To watch the darkness scatter
As sunlight opens the sky.
The day lies clear before me,
All fresh and shining and new,
And then I ask God to guide me
In all that I have to do.

Lord, make me an instrument of your peace.

Where there is hatred, let me sow love;

Where there is injury, pardon;

Where there is discord, union;

Where there is doubt, faith;

Where there is despair, hope;

Where there is darkness, light;

Where there is sadness, joy.

O divine Master, grant that I may
not so much seek to be consoled,
as to console, to be understood, as
to understand, to be loved, as to
love; for it is in giving that we
receive, it is in pardoning that we
are pardoned, and it is in dying
that we are born to eternal life.

Attributed to St Francis of Assisi

Lord Jesus Christ...
fill us with your love
that we may count nothing
too small to do for you,
nothing too much to give,
and nothing too hard to bear.

St Ignatius Loyola

Dear God,

Help me to do good

in the little things that I am allowed to do

so I will know how to do good

when I am allowed to do bigger things.

Dear God,

Ferry me safely across the sea of life:

its calms, its storms,

its shallows, its deeps,

its familiar shoreline and its far horizon.

Dear God,

Help me to be brave enough to risk

adventure and wise enough to stay

out of danger.

Dear God,

Be good to me,

The sea is so wide

And my boat is so small.

Prayer of Breton fishermen

Dear God,

Keep me from going the wrong way, and in your goodness teach me to do what is right.

Based on Psalm 119:29

When
We Are
at Home

Morning is here,
The board is spread,
Thanks be to God,
Who gives us bread.

Anonymous

The Lord is good to me,
And so I thank the Lord
For giving me the things I need,
The sun, the rain, the appleseed.
The Lord is good to me.

Attributed to John Chapman,
American pioneer and planter of orchards

The bread is warm and fresh,
The water cool and clear.
Lord of all life, be with us,
Lord of all life, be near.

African grace

28

For health and strength
and daily food,
we praise your name,
O Lord.

Traditional

All good gifts around us
Are sent from heaven above,
Then thank the Lord, O thank the Lord,
For all his love.

Matthias Claudius,
translated by Jane Montgomery Campbell

Blessed are you, Lord our God,
King of the universe, who feeds
the entire world in his goodness –
with grace, with kindness and with
mercy. He gives food to all life for
his kindness is eternal... Blessed
are you, God, who nourishes all.

Jewish grace

May we have enough food
to satisfy our hunger.
May we be hungry enough
for our food to taste good.

Enjoy the food
but don't be greedy:
Think of those
who are more needy.

Peace be to this house
And to all who dwell in it.
Peace be to them that enter
And to them that depart.

Anonymous

Bless this house which is our home
May we welcome all who come.

Anonymous

Dear God,

When my home is filled with rush and bustle,

Lift the inner me to an island of calm;

When my home is filled with noise and shrieking,

Lift the inner me to an island of calm;

When my home is filled with fighting and
   squabbling,
Lift the inner me to an island of calm.

Then, from my inner calm, give me the
courage to take a little of heaven's quiet grace
back into my muddled old world.

I give thanks for the people
who are my home:
we share a place to shelter;
we share our food;
we share our times of work
and play and rest:
we share our lives.

Dear God,

May this home of ours be like a garden

where, because of our careful and loyal love

and your good grace,

the seeds of hope may grow into

the leaves of kindness and healing,

the flowers of laughter,

the tree of peace

and the fruits of wisdom that will enable

each of us to travel safely to our home

in paradise.

God made the golden sun above,
God made the clear blue sky;
God also made my family,
And here's the question: why?

I think of those I hate to love
and those I love to hate:
help us accept our differences
before it is too late.

I think of the generations of my family
through all the years of time.

I think of how each generation has hoped
that the children will grow up well.

May I, who am the child of them all,
keep faith with God and with myself,
and keep their hope alive.

God bless our sandals
and our sunny days;
God bless our boots
and life's muddy ways;
God bless our shoes
and the days we run:
Bless our journeys
every one.

O God,
Make my way plain before me;
make my way smooth before me;
make my way swift before me;
make my way safe before me.

Please give me courage
for the outward journey;
please give me joy for the
homeward journey.

The home where people love God is
filled with rich and beautiful things.

Based on Proverbs 24:4

When We Are Out and About

Dear God,
May I have a good friend;
may I be a good friend.

A true friend can keep a secret;
but what's the secret of keeping
a true friend?

Dear God,

I have noticed just how often friends let me down.
They don't come along to do the things they
said they'd do, nor do they say the things they
promised to say. Help me to get on with the day
without them, and to bring from it something
different, something good.

O God,

Help our battered

friendships to survive.

Dear God,

Help me to look forward to each school day,

hoping to make discoveries;

help me to look back on every school day,

pleased with what I have learned and understood.

Dear God,

When I don't know the right answer,

please help me ask the right question.

Bullies:
They say, 'We're only teasing.'
But it's not a joke to me.

They say, 'We're only playing.'
But it's not a game to me.

They say, 'We don't mean anything nasty.'
But O God, that's not true.
That's not true.

Who is my neighbour
and who is a stranger?
Whom should I stop for
and who just means danger?
God, give me wisdom
so that I may know
when to be helpful
and when just to go.

Please, God, stay here with me
While I stand and wait.
Someone's meant to fetch me:
Don't let them be late.

In the place where
I live I wish for…

a green open space which is a
little bit wild

and paths that are smooth and safe,
with enough space for old people
   to walk slowly
and toddlers to wobble around
and children to run rather crazily
and nobody to mind a bit…

I pray that the people who live in
it will learn to share the space they
have in a way that is fair, polite and
neighbourly.

Dear God,

Help us to keep wickedness out

of our community:

with the to and fro of ordinary people

who are honest and goodhearted;

with the quiet supervision of the police;

with the prayers of the people of faith.

Dear God,

Be very close to people who have been hurt by crime.

Help them in their shock and helplessness

and shower them with kindness and love.

Dear God,

I pray for those who have no home,

who walk the streets,

who trudge the roads.

I pray for those who want to help them

with the door of welcome

and the meal of companionship

and the bed of rest.

May they be a blessing, the one to the other.

Thank you for the firefighters. High above the ground, in the heat and smoke. Saving lives. Keep them safe, O Lord.

Thank you for the fishermen, their boats tossed by mighty waves and treacherous storms. Bring them home, O Lord.

Thank you for the doctors and nurses. Working through the night. Caring, tending. Comfort them, O Lord.

Thank you for all those who provide for us and give us what we need. Bless them and protect them, O Lord.

Victoria Tebbs

Thank you for the kindhearted
people who serve us in shops and
restaurants and places we visit;
the ones who help us out when we
don't know what to choose and can't
sort out the money really quickly.
Bless them for being polite and patient.

The busy day ends
and people hurry home.
Bring them safely
each and every one
to a place of joy and warmth.

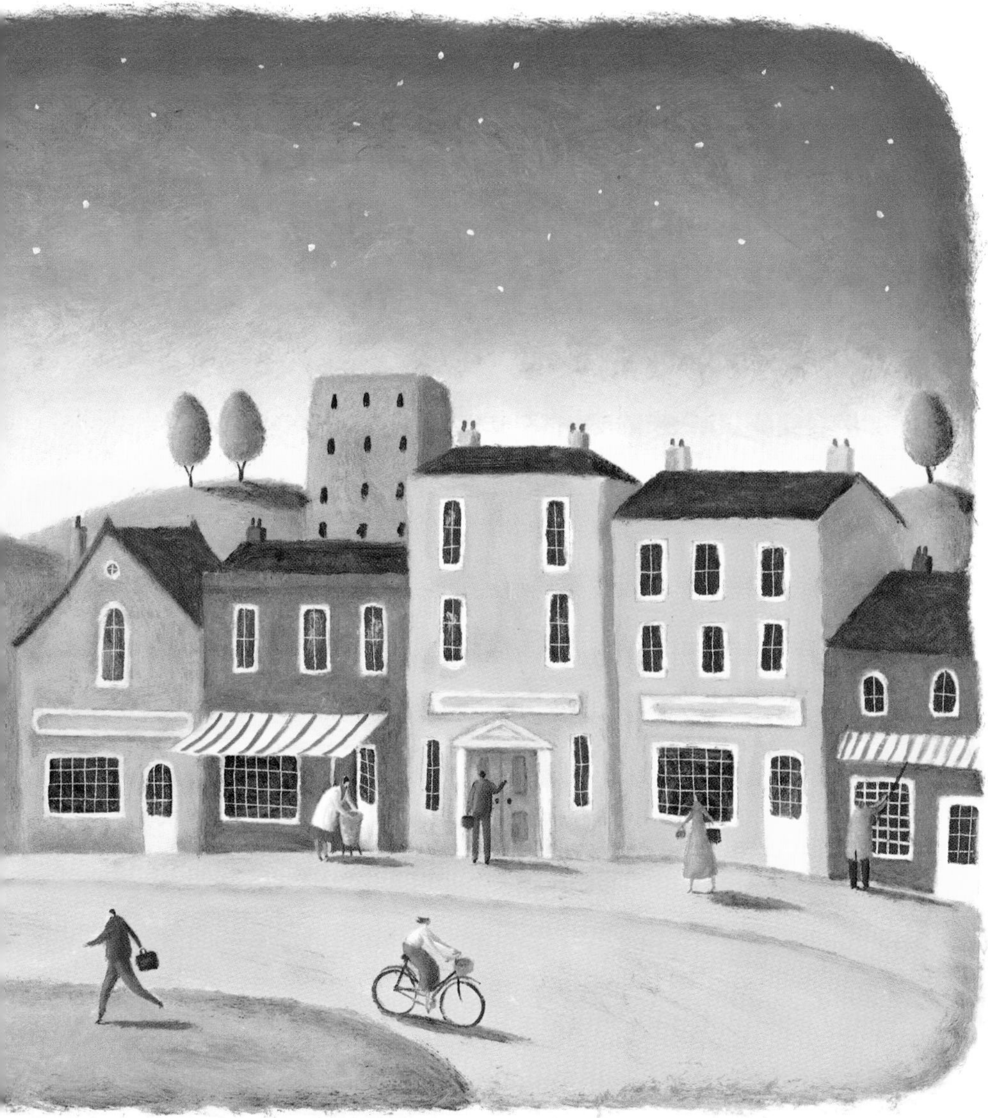

Dear God,

May your goodness and love be with me all my life;
and may your house be my home as long as I live.

Based on Psalm 23:6

We Think About the World

Thank you, dear God,
for the blessing of things that stay
   the same:
for people we have known for ever
and the familiar paths where we walk.

Thank you, dear God,
for the blessing of things that change:
for newcomers with their new customs,
new ways of doing things, new paths
   to discover.

Thank you, dear God,
for the blessing of the old and
   the blessing of the new.

Dear God,
Help me to understand the ways
in which other people are just
like me and to respect them.
Help me to understand the ways
in which other people are quite
different from me and to respect them.

Dear God,

Wherever the children of your world
are at risk or suffering, please send
someone to rescue them: someone strong
and brave who can face the dangers for
them; someone gentle and kind who can
make them feel safe and loved.

Dear God,

Bring us all to a place of safety

in an uncertain world.

Lord, help those who plant and sow,
weed and water, rake and hoe,
toiling in the summer heat
for the food they need to eat.

Bless the work of their tired hands:
turn their dry and dusty lands
to a garden, green and gold,
as their harvest crops unfold.

May the earth be kind to everyone:

pure cool water, flowing;

clean and clear air, blowing;

crops in good earth, growing;

golden sunshine, glowing.

The blessing of rain
The blessing of sun
To all the world
To everyone.

Dear God,

Take care of those who live in war zones:

Afraid of noise,
afraid of silence;

Afraid for themselves,
afraid for others;

Afraid to stay,
afraid to go;

Afraid of living,
afraid of dying.

Give them peace in their hearts,
in their homes
and in their land.

Lord, watch over refugees,
their tired feet aching.
Help them bear their heavy loads,
their backs breaking.
May they find a place of rest,
no fears awake them.
May you always be their guide,
never forsake them.

God does not neglect the poor
and neither will I;
God does not ignore their suffering
and neither will I;
God does not turn away from them
and neither will I;
God answers them when they call for help
and so will I.

Based on Psalm 22:24

We Think About Animals

All things bright and beautiful,
All creatures great and small,
All things wise and wonderful,
The Lord God made them all.

Cecil Frances Alexander

He prayeth best,

   Who loveth best

All things both great and small;

For the dear God

   Who loveth us,

He made and loveth all.

Samuel Taylor Coleridge

God's Care for the Animals

Dear God,

We pray for the animals that run wild:
for their graceful, daring, desperate
dash to survive.

Help us to be gentle with their fear,
respectful of their fierceness,
and wise enough to leave them a place
to live both wild and free.

God's Care for the Animals

God's own peace to the mountains,
God's own peace to the plain:
God's own Paradise garden
Grow in the world again.

Dear God,
Thank you for the animals that have
let us tame them.
Let us learn to understand them
so that they may be at home with us
and us with them.

Dear God,
Help us to love the littlest creatures
you have made:
the beetle on the pathway,
the snail on the doorstep,
and the spider who has come right into
the house without an invitation.
Help us to give each and every one the
space they need.

Evening hush to the barnyard;
Evening hush to the farm;
Evening hush to animals:
Lord, keep them safe from harm.

Make me not too much like the hedgehog:
always prickly;
nor like the rabbit:
always running around;
nor like the goose:
squawking for no good reason;
nor like the fox:
skulking in the shadows.

But rather make me more like the lark:

singing because it is morning;

like the deer:

leaping for the joy of being alive;

like the dolphin:

taking life playfully;

like the seabird:

trusting the power of the invisible.

 $\mathbf{W}$hen I see the birds go soaring,

wheeling, dipping through the sky,

Deep inside my spirit longs to learn to fly.

Like the ox that ploughs so straight
with slow and steady plod
May I learn the humble ways
to live as pleases God.

Dear God,

You have made so many things!

How wisely you made them all!

The earth is filled with your creatures.

Psalm 104:24

This
Fragile
World

Summer sky of blue and white,
Winter sky of grey;
Pink and orange in the dawnlight,
Red at close of day;

Noontime sun of golden yellow,

Moon with silver light:

Sing with gladness for the daytime,

Give thanks for the night.

Mary Joslin

O God,
May the weather be
kind to us
and may we be
kind to the weather.

May the rain fall softly:
no flooding.
May the wind blow gently:
no storm.
May the sun shine brightly:
no burning.
May the weather be kindly
and warm.

On rainy days
I pray for sun.
In burning heat
I dream of snow.
I face the wind
and wish for calm.
I love the sound
when strong winds blow.

And so, dear God,
my prayer is this:
choose the weather
you think is right
for holidays
and for harvest;
for pleasant days
and restful nights.

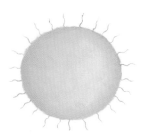

Here on the ancient rock of earth
I sit and watch the sky;
I feel the breeze that moves the trees
While stately clouds float by.
I wonder why our planet home
Spins round and round the sun
And what will last for ever
When earth's days all are done.

Thank you, God, for the good brown soil:
a cradle for each tiny seed;
a home for each growing plant;
a resting place for each fallen leaf.

All praise to the Maker of flowers:
pale flowers, bright flowers;
bold flowers, shy flowers;
long flowers, wide flowers;
tame flowers, wild flowers.

I stand on the sand by the edge
   of the sea
and watch the waves roll by;
I look to the faraway misty line
where water touches sky;

I look at the shapes of the clouds
   in the blue
dissolving into space;
I dream of the heaven where God
   can be found,
where I will see God's face.

Like the river,

I will dance along when I am young.

Like the river,

I will hurry when I am grown.

Like the river,

When I am older I will take my time

Till the tide comes to take me home.

Dear God,

I look at the earth and the sea and the sky

and believe in your everlasting love and strength.

Based on Romans 1:20

Prayers
for
Every
Season

Thank you, God,
for the unchanging
patterns of the seasons:
the frosts of winter
melting into moist spring,
the rain-soaked buds
unfolding into bright summer,

the flowers fading and falling
in the autumn mist
leaving the year cold and bare,
lit by a pale sun
and the golden promise
of your unfailing love.

All is well:

the leaves of grass are growing.

All is well:

the leaves of flowers are showing.

All is well:

the leaves of trees are blowing.

All is well:

God's springtime love is showing.

Thank you, dear God,
for summer days
and summer adventures
and summer holidays so long
it seems that life will go on for ever.

Down by the sea
  is the place I should be
when the summer is sunny and hot;
but now, God, I find myself
  wondering why
in this year the summer is not.

I love to have sand between my toes,
to watch the tide as it comes and goes,
to pick up shells and throw them away:
thank you, dear God, for my holiday.

I love the misty, mysterious days of autumn,
the lingering memories of the summer just gone,
the fond farewells to the summertime birds,
the crackling excitement of the first frosts.

Dear God,

The autumn has come.

Time to look back with thanks.

Time to look forward with courage.

We gather golden sunshine in every harvest grain,
We thank God for the sunshine and for the silver rain.

We thank you, Lord,
for all the riches of autumn:
bronze leaves,
silver spider's webs,
golden harvest.

In winter we see
the world laid bare,
its beauty made clear
in black and white.

Now the wind is coming,

Now the wind is strong,

Now the winter freezes

And the darkness will be long.

Now we see the starlight

In the midnight sky,

We know God is with us

And the angels are close by.

Dear God,
I look at the rainbow
and remember your promise
of summer and winter
and seedtime and harvest
for ever and ever
Amen.

Based on Genesis 8:22, 9:14

Prayers for
the Festivals

Harvest time is gold and red:
Thank you for our daily bread.
Christmas time is red and green:
Heaven now on earth is seen.
Easter time is green and white:
Bring us all to heaven's light.

For all the harvests of the world:
we give you thanks, O God.
For those who work to gather the crops:
we give you thanks, O God.
For those who fill our shops with food:
we give you thanks, O God.
For food to eat and food to share:
we give you thanks, O God.

The harvest of our garden
is astonishingly small;
But oh, dear God, we thank you
that there's anything at all.

In the dark of the year
I will light a candle…

for Christmas, coming soon…

for Jesus, born in Bethlehem…

for the angels' message of peace and
goodwill…

for the star that leads us all to Jesus…

May the light of my Christmas candle
remind me of heaven's light.

Away in a manger, no crib for a bed,
The little Lord Jesus laid down his sweet head.
The stars in the bright sky looked down where
   he lay,
The little Lord Jesus asleep on the hay.

The cattle are lowing, the baby awakes,
But little Lord Jesus no crying he makes.
I love thee, Lord Jesus! Look down from the sky,
And stay by my side until morning is nigh.

Be near me, Lord Jesus; I ask thee to stay

Close by me for ever, and love me, I pray.

Bless all the dear children in thy tender care,

And fit us for heaven, to live with thee there.

Traditional

Dear God,

May our Christmas be your Christmas.

Let us give and receive gifts with love.

Let us feast on friendship and forgiveness.

Let us decorate not just with tinsel

But with the light that shines from heaven.

The stars that shine at Christmas
Shine on throughout the year;
Jesus, born so long ago,
Still gathers with us here.
We listen to his stories,
We learn to say his prayer,
We follow in his footsteps
And learn to love and share.

Lord Jesus, who died upon the cross:
You know this world's suffering,
You know this world's sorrowing,
You know this world's dying.

In your name, Lord Jesus, who rose again:
I will work for this world's healing,
I will work for this world's rejoicing,
I will work for this world's living.

In the Easter garden
the leaves are turning green;
in the Easter garden
the risen Lord is seen.

In the Easter garden
we know that God above
brings us all to heaven
through Jesus and his love.

Dear God,

Be close to me

in the rushing wind,

and make me bold to do good.

Be close to me

in the golden fire,

and help me to deeds

of shining goodness.

A Pentecost prayer

Dear God,

Thank you for the example of other Christians. From the stories of their faith, may I grow in understanding. From the stories of their kindhearted deeds, may I learn to do good.

Dear God,

You welcome us into your presence.

May we never forget to gather to

worship you.

Based on Leviticus 23:3

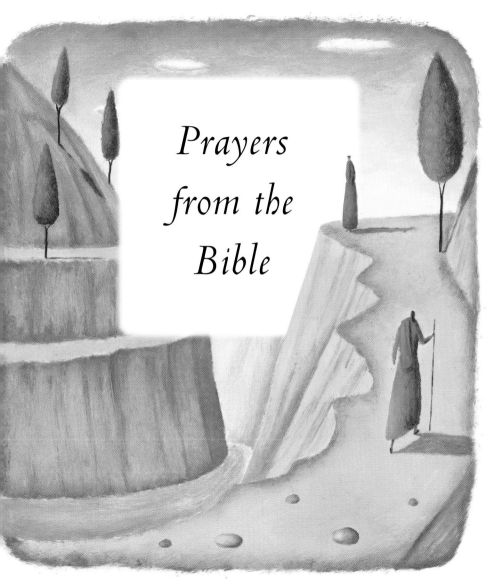

Prayers
from the
Bible

All the angels dance and sing,
Gifts of song to God they bring;
Praising God who made the earth,
Praising God who gave us birth.

Based on Psalm 148

Shine through the night, O silvery moon,
Shine through the day, O you sun,
Shine in the dark, you glittering stars,
To praise what your Maker has done.

Based on Psalm 148

Praise the Lord, all nations!
Praise him, all peoples!
His love for us is strong
and his faithfulness is eternal.
Praise the Lord!

Psalm 117

Sing a new song to the Lord!
Sing to the Lord, all the world!
Sing to the Lord, and praise him!

Psalm 96:1–2

Dear God,

Keep me from worrying;

for you have promised

that when your people pray to you

with thanksgiving

you will hear them

and will help them.

Based on Philippians 4:6

Protect me, O God; I trust in you for safety.

Psalm 16:1

Answer me now, Lord!

Remind me each morning of your constant love,

for I put my trust in you.

My prayers go up to you;

show me the way I should go.

Psalm 143:7, 8

Let us love one another,
because love comes from God.
Whoever loves is a child of God
and knows God.

1 John 4:7

Dear God, you are my shepherd,
You give me all I need;
You take me where the grass grows green
And I can safely feed.

You take me where the water
Is quiet and cool and clear;
And there I rest and know I'm safe
For you are always near.

Based on Psalm 23

How I love you, Lord!
You are my defender.
The Lord is my protector;
he is my strong fortress.

Psalm 18:1–2

The Lord is my light and my salvation;

I will fear no one.

The Lord protects me from all danger;

I will never be afraid.

Psalm 27:1

When I lie down, I go to sleep in peace;
you alone, O Lord, keep me perfectly safe.

Psalm 4:8

May the grace of the Lord Jesus Christ, and the love of God, and the fellowship of the Holy Spirit be with us all, evermore.

Based on 2 Corinthians 13:13

Our Father, who art in heaven,
hallowed be thy name;
thy kingdom come;
thy will be done;
on earth as it is in heaven.
Give us this day our daily bread.
And forgive us our trespasses,
as we forgive those who trespass against us.
And lead us not into temptation;
but deliver us from evil.
For thine is the kingdom, the power,
and the glory, for ever and ever. Amen.

A traditional version, based on Matthew 6:9–13 and Luke 11:2–4

God loves you, so don't let anything
worry you or frighten you.

Daniel 10:19

Prayers
for
Sad Times

All that we ought to have thought and have
not thought,
All that we ought to have said and have
not said,
All that we ought to have done and have
not done,

All that we ought not to have spoken and
   yet have spoken,
All that we ought not to have done, and
   yet have done,
For these words, and works, pray we,
   O God, for forgiveness.

Traditional

I think of the careless accidents
That ruin a perfect day:
The china vase that I just let fall,
The stain I can't wash away.

I pray to the God of all mending
To bring some good from the mess

So once again things will be all right
And I'll know in my heart I am blessed.

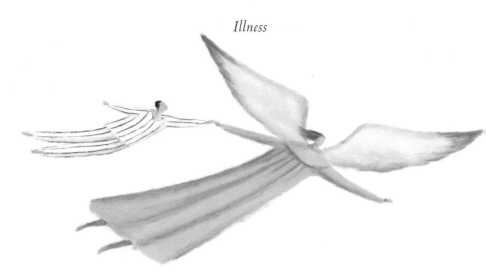

Dear God, my head is hurting,
Dear God, my head is sore,
Dear God, I really don't think
I can stand it any more.

Dear God, please make me better,
Dear God, be swift to heal,
Dear God, you surely understand
Just how unwell I feel.

Dear God,
I've been injured.
I've been wounded.
I've been hurt.
I've been damaged.

I want to be
mended,
patched,
fixed,
healed.

Dear God,
When the outside me
gets hurt and bruised,
people who love me
can wrap me in softness.

When the inside me
gets hurt and bruised,
only you can wrap me
in softness.

I dare not say anything
about the things that frighten me,
about the people who hurt me,
about how I get pushed around.

But now I am telling my silent nothing
so it can be shouted aloud in heaven –
aloud, aloud, aloud, aloud:
till someone on earth hears my cry.

Dear God,

When sadness brings me to tears,

Give me space and time to weep.

Dear God,

Be with me in the dark:

through the night-time dark of shadows;

through the daytime dark of sadness.

Amen.

Help me to say this last goodbye.
Give me a quiet place to cry.

Dear God,

Into your care we give this little creature who has died.

We lay a green leaf beside her, and remember her life.

We lay a brown leaf beside her, and mourn her death.

We scatter a handful of petals to the gentle wind

and trust that the life that has blown away from us

will be safe with you.

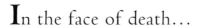

In the face of death…

I want to run away.

I want to stay close.

I want to shout in anger.

I want to sit in silence.

I want to toss my head and not care.

I want to weep till I have no more tears.

In the face of death, dear God, I don't
know what to do.

I believe in the sun even when it is not shining

I believe in love where feeling is not

I believe in God even if he is silent.

Inscription on the walls of a cellar in Cologne, Germany, where Jews hid from the Nazis

In the face of evil and wrongdoing
I will surely not be happy,
Nor will I let myself grow too sad.
Instead, I will choose to stand up for what is right
And I will face the future
With calm and courage and cheerfulness.

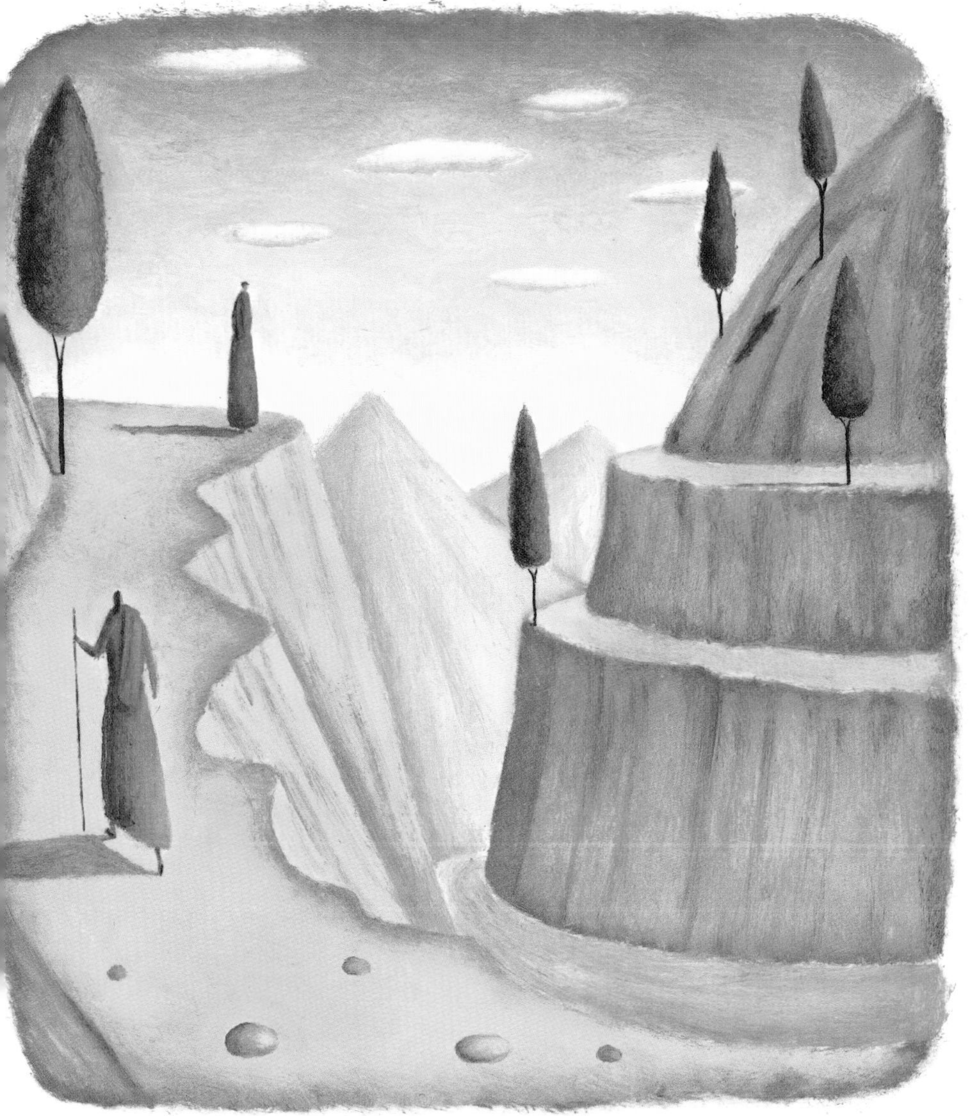

Dear God,
I wait for your help
in my time of sadness
as eagerly as I wait for the dawn
to scatter the dark of night.

Based on Psalm 130:5–6

Prayers
for Quiet
Times

In the place which is my home
Is a space all of my own
Where God comes to talk with me:
My home for eternity.

O God, make us children of quietness,
and heirs of peace.

St Clement of Alexandria

Here I am beneath the sky
and all alone in prayer;
but I know God is listening,
for God is everywhere.

God, who made the earth,
The air, the sky, the sea,
Who gave the light its birth,
Careth for me.

God, who made the grass,
The flower, the fruit, the tree,
The day and night to pass,
Careth for me.

God, who made all things,
On earth, in air, in sea,
Who changing seasons brings,
Careth for me.

Sarah Betts Rhodes

Loving Shepherd of Thy sheep,
Keep Thy lambs, in safety keep;
Nothing can Thy power withstand;
None can pluck us from Thy hand.

Jane Eliza Leeson

Jesus, friend of little children,
Be a friend to me;
Take my hand, and ever keep me
Close to thee...

Never leave me, nor forsake me;
Ever be my friend;
For I need thee, from life's dawning
To its end.

Walter John Mathams

Here in this calm and quiet place
I can just sit and stay
To think my thoughts and say my prayers
As daylight slips away.
I look to where earth touches sky
And hope that I will see
Beyond the edges of this world
To where God waits for me.

Dear God,
There are some things I do
which really aren't worth the time;
and some things I don't do
which I know I should.
Even as I say this prayer
I can see that I need
to make some changes.

May I have joy in my heart.

May I find joy in my life.

May I bring joy to others.

May I spread joy through the world.

God, who touchest earth with beauty,
Make me lovely too;
With thy Spirit recreate me,
Make my heart anew.

Like thy springs and running waters,
Make me crystal pure;
Like thy rocks of towering grandeur,
Make me strong and sure.

Like thy dancing waves in sunlight,
Make me glad and free;
Like the straightness of the pine-trees
Let me upright be.

Mary S. Edgar

God Hears My Prayer

I travel this world by sunlight,

seeing the way I should go;

I travel this world by moonlight,

trusting its silvery glow;

I travel this world by starlight,

trusting in heaven above;

I walk through this old world's darkness,

safe in the light of God's love.

Dear God,

May I hear you speaking

in the soft whisper of a voice.

Based on 1 Kings 19:12

Prayers

for the

Night

Now the day is over,
Night is drawing nigh,
Shadows of the evening
Steal across the sky.

Now the darkness gathers,
Stars begin to peep;
Birds and beasts and flowers
Soon will be asleep.

Sabine Baring-Gould

Who made the night-time shadows?
Who made the silver stars?
Who made the moon that floats on high
Where clouds and angels are?

The One who made the morning sun,
The daytime sky of blue,
The One who made both you and me
And loves both me and you.

Sophie Piper

200

Glory to Thee, my God, this night
For all the blessings of the light;
Keep me, O keep me, King of kings,
Beneath Thy own almighty wings.

Praise God, from whom all blessings flow;
Praise him, all creatures here below;
Praise him above, ye heavenly host;
Praise Father, Son, and Holy Ghost.

Bishop Thomas Ken

God bless all those that I love;
God bless all those that love me;
God bless all those that love those that I love
and all those that love those that love me.

New England sampler

Tucked up in my little bed
I say a little prayer
For all the people in this house
And people everywhere.

Sophie Piper

I climb into my soft bed
and remember those whose life is hard;
I snuggle under my warm quilt
and remember those whose life is cold;
I lay my head upon my pillow
and pray that you will give us all rest.

Peace of the running waves to you,

Deep peace of the flowing air to you,

Deep peace of the quiet earth to you,

Deep peace of the shining stars to you,

Deep peace of the shades of night to you,

Moon and stars always giving light to you,

Deep peace of Christ, the Son of Peace, to you.

Traditional Gaelic blessing

Be thou a bright flame before me,

Be thou a guiding star above me,

Be thou a smooth path below me,

Be thou a kindly shepherd behind me,

Today, tonight, and for ever.

From Carmina Gadelica

Preserve us, O Lord, while waking
and guard us while sleeping;
that awake we may watch with Christ,
and asleep we may rest in peace.

Traditional

Now I lay me down to sleep,
I pray thee, Lord, thy child to keep;
Thy love to guard me through the night
And wake me in the morning light.

Traditional

Lord, keep us safe this night,
Secure from all our fears;
May angels guard us while we sleep,
Till morning light appears.

John Leland

Prayers for the Night

Goodnight

Day is done,
Gone the sun
From the lake,
From the hills,
From the sky.
Safely rest,
All is well!
God is nigh.

Anonymous

The moon shines bright,
The stars give light
Before the break of day;
God bless you all,
Both great and small,
And send a joyful day.

Anonymous

Dear God,

Watch over me through the sunlit day;

protect me through the moonlit night.

Based on Psalm 121:5–6

First Line Index

Loving Shepherd of Thy sheep 186

Make me not too much like the hedgehog 84
May I have joy in my heart 191
May the earth be kind to everyone 66
May the grace of the Lord Jesus Christ 157
May the rain fall softly 93
May we have enough food 31
Morning is here 26

Now I lay me down to sleep 210
Now the day is over 198
Now the wind is coming 121

O God, Help our battered 45
O God, Make my way plain before me 41

Thank you, dear God, for summer days 110

Thank you, dear God, for the blessing of
   things that stay the same 60

Thank you for the firefighters 54

Thank you for the kindhearted people 55

Thank you for this new day 13

Thank you, God, for the good brown soil 98

Thank you, God, for the unchanging 106

Thank you, God in heaven 12

The blessing of rain 67

The bread is warm and fresh 28

The busy day ends 56

The harvest of our garden 127

The home where people love God is 42

The Lord is good to me 28